Other titles in the UWAP Poetry series (established 2016)

T0363947

Scratchland

Noëlle Janaczewska

Noëlle Janaczewska is a poet, playwright, essayist, and the author of *The Book of Thistles* (UWA Publishing, 2017). Her writing has been produced, broadcast and published locally and internationally, and in 2014 she received a prestigious Windham-Campbell Prize from Yale University for her body of work as a dramatist. In Australia Noëlle's plays and audio scripts have won a Queensland Premier's Literary Award, the Playbox-Asialink Playwriting Competition, the Griffin Award, and ten AWGIE (Australian Writers' Guild Industry Excellence) Awards. Noëlle also presents performance essays, a term she coined to describe a hybrid which mashes the essay and the monologue with other sources and genres. These include *The Hannah First Collection, 1919-1949*, created for the Zendai Museum of Modern Art in Shanghai and *Blasted Island—Nauru's backstory* for the Sydney Opera House Festival of Dangerous Ideas. Noëlle's poems have been performed live, set to music, and broadcast on ABC Radio National. They have appeared in anthologies and literary journals, in feature films and artists' books. *Scratchland* is her first collection.

Noëlle Janaczewska
Scratchland
scenarios & solos from
a mixed landscape

true crimers

Poetry

First published in 2020 by
UWA Publishing
Crawley, Western Australia 6009
www.uwap.uwa.edu.au

UWAP is an imprint of UWA Publishing,
a division of The University of Western Australia.

Copyright © Noëlle Janaczewska 2020
The moral right of the author has been asserted.
ISBN: 978-1-76080-144-1

A catalogue record for this
book is available from the
National Library of Australia

Designed by Becky Chilcott, Chil3
Typeset in Lyon Text by Lasertype
Printed by McPherson's Printing Group

 uwapublishing

MIX
Paper from
responsible sources
FSC www.fsc.org FSC® C001695

Contents

Scratchland /skrætʃlænd/ ▸ **noun** the wild frontiers of our urban centres.
■ A place of random, and perhaps not so random, encounters where some of the people, creatures and stuff surplus to requirements in our society wash up.

Scenarios & solos from a mixed landscape

Power lines, a storage clerk & buzzing insects

Cappuccino, two-sugar,
roast beef-on-Turkish.

Camphor laurels,
the asphalt cracks up.

Movement of goods
through jagged quotas.

I take my takeaway
and take it out here.

The buzz of power lines
honey bees fall out of hives.

I take my phone
and take a break.

Self and storage
words that shouldn't go together.

Sometimes I wonder
what on earth are we keeping?

More buzz, this time blowflies
that's where she was.

I didn't cross the line
the line crossed me.

A child, a car park attendant & an imaginary wolf called Barry

Eucs. Frags. Criss-cross.
Ivy-drivel. Fuck-grass.
Sweetbitter. Twigshadow.
Pigface. Troublemaker.
Ratbag. Dizzle. Bugger-plant.

> She gives the plants names
> the man unzips
> his backpack
> pulls out bread and humus
>
> offers tomatoes the size of marbles
> to the little girl with eyelashes
> pale as wood shavings
> who smells of wee and neglect.

Piss kids. Dirt kids. Scared kids.
Bullied kids. Never-go-to-school kids.
Druggie's kids. Kids called Elvis.
Patched-up kids. Shut-the-fuck-up kids.
Old-before-their-time kids.

> *I'm not allowed—*
> *you won't tell will you Mister?*
> *I'll get a whack from Bob*
> *and a smack from Mum*

and the bitch next door
will call the cops
then Bob will go berserko
he hates when people call the cops

Bob's my uncle
Barry's my friend he's a wolf
have you got anything else to eat?
Barry's starving—he likes Coco Pops.

Snap. Crack. Sugar high.
Chatterbox. Forget-me-nots.
Dummy-weed. Prickle-backs.

A solitary crow rides the current
jet plumage reflecting a trail
of oily light.

The man knows enough
to know his kindness
to Meli—that's her name
will attract suspicion

the child knows enough
to know that for grown-ups
like Gürkan—that's his name
Barry is invisible.

There's a ghost lives here
I've seen it
like a normal ghost
but sweaty

I've never seen a ghost sweating
have you Mister?
rattling chains going woo-hoo
but not sweaty.

They laugh
the car park attendant and the child
and the moments
follow each other

and now his day has a skip in it
Istanbul comes back to him
hanging out in Cihangir
before it got trendy

chatting to the silk-flower seller
running his fingers over
tuberoses and lilacs
stunned by the quality of imitation.

What does God smell like?
I think it's cheese
God smells
like cheese.

Puff. Piffle. Pap.
Killer cereal. Monster in the box.
Snap. Crackle. Cops.

Cyclists whoosh by
buddlejas nod their clotted blooms
nothing is suddenly black and white.

People protect one another
that's how it is
they see something they don't understand
they think it must be a mistake

human beings are like that
that's how it is
the good in people which stops
them saying what they know

but the thing people often forget about
the story of *The Boy Who cried Wolf*
is that, at the end of the day
there was a wolf.

Dumped carpet

I spy round midnight
two blokes dumping
what might be
probably is in fact
an old carpet.
But there's something
about the way it rolls
how it hangs between them...
See the motif
Persian or Turkish
and then they're gone.
Like the place swallowed them up.

To be honest
this is dark stuff.
Tap roots insinuate
shoots seek underworlds.
Grapeskins and the cheesy stink
of two-for-one pizza.
Crime dramas with spaghetti
plots, splash of sci-fi.
Something human something heavy
its wool caked in mud, blood, whatever
and from the tube emerges a wolf.
It shifts the shape of the story.

Imaginary wolf

You're looking at an empty fridge, a
busted window, a threadbare mother—
that's where I come in. I'm the children's
bedtime, the once upon a time, I'm where the story
pulls away from the forest. Listen! Hear that
growling? Is it a dog? The Ipswich train? Is it
a bass clarinet?—that's my favourite instrument,
by the way. The fabric of life is very stretchy,
but still—Don't talk to strangers. Or strays.
Don't be tempted by ice-cream. Find
a responsible adult. Put them in a line-up
and no two words are truly identical,
a feline isn't always a cat. Speaking of which—
Hate tigers, really do, attention-stealing stripy buggers.
You're looking again at that empty fridge, the
busted window, the threadbare mother—
I'm the wolf at the door, the shadow in the corner
of your eye. I'm the fiction in the wardrobe, devourer
of stars, pelt soft as moonlight. There's no rhyme
to my reason but I know the way through
the woods. Oh, what big teeth I have!
More growling, and here we are, a no-go zone
whose outlawed areas change every day. Warning
signs, knee-jerks, bindweeds, the stillness
kicks in. Sometimes I worry about reality, I really do.
There's no explanation, no fairy tale to fill the gap,
only the physical presence of the little girl.

An improvised allotment & a migrant from francophone Africa

Drained, infenced
chillies, okra, a geometry of cabbage
no, she doesn't have permission
the land was an incidental wilderness
why not use it?
It's good growing
this rivered earth.
Plastic bag rubbish, dead TVs, things
you'd rather not think about
cleared to make the plot.
The wire she stitched together
to keep out the wild dogs
left to their own devices
foraging and wandering
like we all do to survive.

After work she comes here
with newspapers customers left behind
sits bare feet in the water
reads headlines about the world's
twenty-second richest man.
Does anyone know the name
of the twenty-second poorest person in the world?

> *Well hi there. I'm Monique Sawadogo. What's your name?*
> *Sawadogo means cloud and we like clouds*
> *because they bring the rain.*
> *Never realised it rained so much in Australia—*
> *this bit of it anyway.*

The inside-land is more like where I come from.
You'll never guess no one ever does
and even when I tell them
they still don't know. It's landlocked
and more or less flat like here.

It used to be called Haute-Volta
Upper Volta. *A former colony*
of French West Africa. The name was changed
to Burkina Faso because we're a lot more
than a location on the River Volta.

But it's still the same impoverished land
filled with wind like the music I listen to
savannahs that became deserts
water that doesn't exist. It's a vulnerable
country. Dry Volta. Hungry Volta. Unstable Volta.

Now the French are gone
but their language remains
Regardez là-bas, c'est un piano jouet.

My father was a chief
postman. My mother had a cabbage
farm but it got eaten by moths.

If you're a cabbage
the tiny
diamondback moth
is massive.
Munching through
acres of cruciferous crops.
Enter a moth
with engineered DNA.
Biotech company says
better these GM insects
than chemical sprays.
Opponents say
once released
Frankenmoths are
for ever.

I'm a blood group, a skin colour
the face on the charity ad: Sponsor a Child Today.
I'm a student visa, a food court worker
wiper of tables, stacker of trays
I'm beside the plot, beside a creek the colour of beer bottles.

The colonial patchwork of West Africa is gone
but waves still break on coasts
called Grain, Ivory, Gold and Slave.

Burkina Faso, is that a country?
This guy from my science ed. class thought
it sounded like the name of a world music singer

we laughed
and life tick-tocked.

The cabbages are growing up
I don't mind if people help themselves
one or two but it makes me mad
when someone smashes them for the sake of it.
If you'd ever been hungry you wouldn't do that.

The girl who's not here

Los Angeles energised me
people find the place obnoxious
but I liked the sunshine
the buildings, even the trees
seemed optimistic.

A hundred different countries
packed into a single traffic jam
but I liked the driving
the canyon roads, hood down
pretending you're a movie star.

>   *How r u going over there?*
>   *Give us a call, Mum. Kiss, kiss.*

Phone rings
murder victim in a Netflix series
interview tomorrow.
Tell us about yourself, your family
where you come from.

Our house
mid-range Mitsubishi in the drive
lawn, Labrador, coffee tables
totally tragic
in our ordinariness.

Miss u, sweetheart. Storms in Brisbane.
Call me when u get this, love Mum.

Another week another audition
another girl meets boy meets violent end
I get a call back
it's touch and go for a while
then more go than touch.

PS saw Niko in the supermarket. x

Niko. The short version.
A seventeen-year-old
and a twenty-year-old
meet in a boring pub
in a boring suburb.

Two people with dreams
similar but different
she wants to act
after almost a year
the event to be avoided happens.

We have to get rid of it.
No, he says. This is what I want
the sunbeam to end all sunbeams
their words swim past each other

the boy comes round
the girl's parents pay
so their daughter won't have to
everybody moves on.

      Nana Vas died last night.
      Call us a.s.a.p. love Mum.

She was my last grandparent
hadn't seen her for yonks
and to be brutally honest
she was a bit of a cow

the other grandparents went
a while ago in quick succession
cancer, heart attack
the usual boring illnesses.

I wanted something more exotic
Niko's granddad died
from a tropical disease
he picked up in Africa

but then Niko's family
were that sort of family
mine die from old age
or complications.

Do u need $ for a flight home?
Let me know sweetheart, love Mum.

Confirming tomorrow 5:45
rock up, play the part
one scene, two lines, three minutes
running away from a serial killer.

At Starbucks the staff are all in character
there's something about LA
that turns everyone into actors
pining for the role you can't have.

Call us Avril.
We worry about u over there. x

I see girls like you
the last casting agent said
with lovely photogenic faces
but you've come to a city
that's standing room only.

Give it six months, a year
and you're broken
by the weight of possibility.
Then you've got two options—
porn or the hell out.

I texted Mum.

Floodwater, a bunch of soggy menus & an old Beatles song

River has broken
go for a ride   fill in a form

Warnings are current
lights have gone   lock the door

Rainfall is falling
dry curry   heavenly braised

Story starts at sixty-four
flaky pockets filled with mixture

Small and large options
beware debris washed down

                    Snakes sides specials with soup
                                    or no soup
                swamp, sinkholes, additional toppings—

                    Rip rap run from the trollshapes
                                under the bridge
                Diet Coke, Classic, No sugar, Pepsi hates Coke—

                    Threat is real authorities
                            open the floodgates
                people, pets, crows gather for flight—

Know this haemorrhage of water
for what it is

Tugged by the tide
mud-spackle   battered fish   drop me a line

Among windblown reeds
a chirpy Beatles song about getting older

Filling buckets hefting sandbags
the narratives that keep us home and dry.

Toy factory worker

Lyrics to be sung in a sentimental key.

Wei Lanfen went to Toyland
thought she had her future planned.

Wei Lanfen dons cap and mask
nineteen years old and worn out.

Wei Lanfen stamps out doll parts
untold thousands every day.

Opens the machine.
Coughs.
Puts in the plastic
presses the machine
takes out the plastic.
Coughs again.

Factory air is fuzzy.
Chemicals.
Protective gear
slows her down
so she works bare-hands.
Chemicals again.

Wei Lanfen works nightmare hours
sunlight almost a forgotten thing.

Wei Lanfen can't swallow any more
but the cost of leaving is out of reach.

Wei Lanfen went to Toyland
thought she had her future planned...

Unregistered plot

It's dirty
no point denying it
there's talk, there's always talk.

Where the road
loops round and back
going nowhere, like a kid's train set.

A secret
you have to know about
to know about.

He's a cark park attendant
all the way from Istanbul
counting coins, lifting the bar, listening to
thirty-odd reasons why
he's wrong, the system's wrong—
Go on, I dare you!

She's M-E-L-I no E
from somewhere vaguely over there
her toys at home are obvious pink
one of the reasons why
she likes it better here—
Come on, come closer!

Hear the hiss of rancid mattress
snap of rotten weatherboard
see the morning glories with their purple trumpets

twists of dog rose flash of cycle-past—
it's all about cycling now isn't it?
Gotta make the world safe for cyclists.

People get caught
carried by the tide of life
in directions they never intended.

Buddleja

Butterflies love me. Just love, love, love me.
Those sweet things can't get enough of my honey.

My name comes from the Latin
B-U-double D-L-E-J-A. Buddleja
it was given to me by Linnaeus himself
to honour an English clergyman and naturalist
called Adam Buddle who compiled
one of those massive herbaria
they were into back then.

Loads of ministers took up botanising
I guess because, A, they had time on their hands
and B, they believed studying plants
would bring them closer to God. Or something.
So I'm buddleja, a.k.a. butterfly bush, summer lilac, et cetera
I sort of rhyme with with idea, sangria and Sofia
but you can call me buddy.

Did I mention that I'm a butterfly magnet?
Bees and moths also find me pretty attractive.

My story comes from the warmer regions
Asia, Africa and the Americas
but I've migrated all over the place.
My colour comes from my easy-going nature
and ability to adapt.
Flower spikes dangle over walls, lurch from brickwork
push up from rubble and birdshit.

I'm your garden variety, but don't call me common
I'm not common, and I resent the description
I'm cultivated.
There's a lot of breeding in me
my particular ancestry is Chinese.
Buddleja davidii in italics is my full name
the davidii bit commemorates a French missionary.

(Same bloke who shipped the first live panda back to Europe.
Where it starved to death because no one knew what to feed it.)

I arrived in London's Kew Gardens, via Paris, in 1896
thanks to another itinerant priest
yeah, yeah, there's a lot of religion in my history.
Anyway that particular priest
came to an unfortunate end.
He was tortured and shot by Tibetan monks
so much for harmony and nonviolence.

Enviros—that's what I call eco-warriors and suchlike
enviros might tut-tut, but really!
what's not to love about me?
OK, my ways are brazen and I accept
that some people don't like that in a plant.
But I'm also tenacious, fast-growing, not fussy about where
see how my purple softens slag heaps and bombsites.

I'm inner city I'm bush and everything in-between.
I'm a twentieth century super-shrub.

Once I put down roots I'm pretty undemanding
I may appear all delicate and lacy
but we buddlejas are long lived.
We survive deluge and drought
soul-shivering frosts and suburban make-overs.
We flourish where other plants
give up the ghost.

My seeds volunteer themselves everywhere—I know, I know
that's why there's all that drama about keeping me out
but hasn't a buddleja got organs, dimensions, sensitivities?
Aren't we fed by the same soil
warmed and cooled by the same winter and summer?
If you poison us, we die
if you cut us, do we not sprout anew?

I'm a self-starter with an erotic and salty life
suck on my nectar, hover flies and ladybirds!
Do not, not, not curse my tribe
I belong here as much as the gums
as much as cockatoos and wattle
unlike that body, not moving
attracting its own insect life.

Mermaids' tears & a washed up doll

A broken arm
a slur of nail varnish
the sparkle of broken glass.

Shattered fleabane
empty stockings
a lifetime's subscription to *National Geographic*.

Detection of chlorine on the body indicates that it's most likely
composed of PVC or polyvinyl chloride to give it its scientific
name. Also present are carbon and hydrogen, as well as amounts
of plasticisers, stabilisers and other additives. You'll notice that
although it's been here for a while, the limbs are still flexible. That's
down to those agents and additives.

There are deep scratches on the thighs and a bite mark on the right
shoulder. Possibly from a dog.

Plastics like PVC last a very long time because the chemical
connectors that hold the molecules together are generally stronger
than nature's power to take them apart. The insects and micro-
organisms that decompose organic material won't touch this stuff.

The only real way to break down plastic is through photo-degrading—
which requires sunlight. When UV rays strike plastic, they break the
bonds holding its molecular chain together. Over time, a lot of time,
this turns an individual into a load of tiny beads called nurdles or
mermaids' tears.

Takes five-hundred
to a thousand years
for this body's plastic self to disappear.

Grease and gristle
solvents and solutions
the ferment of the marketplace froths up.

Styrofoam

Imagine Isaac Newton
leaning against an apple tree
that day in 1665 or 6—

Imagine another windfall
Midland, Michigan
that day in 1940-something—

Researchers at Dow Chemical found
a way to make foamed polystyrene
stamped it with their brand and voilà
Styrofoam was born.

It packs up and insulates
cushions and fills voids

helps you refloat your boat
or arrange flowers.

Prisoners at Guantanamo Bay
weren't allowed pens or paper
so they used stones

and scratched messages
into the Styrofoam cups
they got with their meals.

When the guards weren't looking
they passed the cups between cells
not escape plans or jihadi plots
they were swapping poems.

Imagine an outlet
nothing flowery.

Imagine particles
exhaling toxins

and you understand
the gravity of the situation.

Random grasses & a cautionary tale about a side-striped jackal

Which do you like best
leaves or flowers?
I like leaves.
Are you scared
of spiders?
I'm not
but lots of people
are frightened.
I'm Meli and this is Barry
is that watermelon?
When I'm grown up
my family will eat
Coco Pops every meal.

Sedge, rush and bristle
creeping and weeping
syllables flicker
stems bend
clouds pass.
Panic—

Large panic grass a.k.a. Guinea grass
is of African origin
likewise feather and fountain
mission and molasses
elephant and gamba grass.

The acclimatising gentlemen of Australia
called Guinea grass a miracle plant.
Said the chaps who introduced it deserved
statues illuminated by night
and visible throughout colony.

Meli says she like stories
with animals that talk
so Monique tells her the tale
of the side-striped jackal
and Meli grows quiet in her shadow.

Now and then
more then than now
from a time when watches had hands
there's a lion stuck in a cage
and he wants to escape.

When an old woman walks past
the lion calls out to her:
Will you let me out of this cage?
The old woman shakes her head.
Oh, please, please, please, let me out.

I'm sorry you're locked up,
says the old woman, but I'm afraid
that if I let you out you'll eat me.
No, I won't, says the lion, I really truly won't.
So the woman opens the cage door.

No sooner is he released
than the lion leaps at the old woman,
who screams and runs away
as fast as she can—
which isn't actually very fast at all.

The lion is about to grab the woman
when a side-striped jackal
appears on the scene.
Let's ask the side-striped jackal
if you should eat me, suggests the old woman.

The lion explains that
although he'd kind of promised
not to eat the old woman,
he's incredibly hungry, starving in fact.
I don't understand, says the side-striped jackal.

The lion repeats his explanation
the jackal still doesn't get it.
Look, says the lion,
I was trapped in a cage,
and I asked this old woman to let me out.

Show me, says the jackal.
Like this, says the lion
and gets into the cage to demonstrate.
Quick as a flash the jackal
slams the door and locks it.

The jackal and the old woman walk away
and by way of thank you for saving her
from becoming the lion's lunch
the side-striped jackal is rewarded
with a feast of his favourite food.

Crow

Remember my face and voice because I'll certainly remember yours.
Up I fly to scan this lip of land and yes, see the bigger picture
Oh, you poor landlocked bipeds
if you could see what I see...

There's the dead end where Caleb Stevens of 71 Holland Terrace
    crashed the motorbike he borrowed from outside the Red Lion
    Hotel.
That's the gravel where Gürkan Solok spilt a tub of hummus
and there's the missing girl's missing shoe.

I'm no bird brain, I'm bright-eyed and smart in ways you can't
    imagine. You primates with your wi-fi and wars.
And of course I can fly—an ability you've always envied.
I know what's coming, I saw it happen...

Away the bush runs, in and out of pale suburbs, emerging then swept
    away.
Where worker bees swarm and you're never more than a peck away
    from a stray French-fry or two.
Sad when farms are sacrificed
to mining interests.

Happy early mornings before the traffic.
Likewise winter nights when the air punches in from the Pacific.
All lost to you in the cocoon
of your four-wheel drives.

I play tricks and hide things.
I stole an engagement ring.
Hid it under some rotting leaves.
Why?—'cause I like shiny elements.

After the Great Fire of London I fed on cadavers. Cycle of life. What's
    yuk to you is supper for me.
And here's a thing: I like to eavesdrop conversations.
Certain—let's call them authoritarian governments—have recruited
    me to spy on suspect citizens.
Comrades!
See how the crow flies over the capital.
Hear the beating of its wings.
See it take off with your whispered words and furthest thoughts.

I know this place with its flashy lorikeets and fried chicken shops.
The body in the buddleja.
I know its dirty secrets, its knock-off shops, knocking shops, knock-
    knock who's there?
Is it Bob the bricklayer?—No! Wait, it's Ashley Park PhD with TV
    crews
and sniffing dogs searching for clues
picking up scraps of cellophane and cigarette ends. Hey, leave some
    butts for me—I use them to smoke out parasites
the ticks that live under my wings. Recycling, gotta love it, eh?
When the scientists get too close for comfort I stick my black arse out
over the edge of the branch and crap in their face.
Nothing like a bit of avian revenge.

Yes, I eat babies. Baby rabbits, rodents, the odd yabby.
I plunder nests and swallow filth.
I think in the key of *Corvus*
and I've starred in a shitload of poems and memoirs.

I pluck a nice bit of liver from a wallaby road-killed in the temporary
    car-park
and carry it to the top of the stringybark
growing next to that public-sculpture-concrete-thingy.
Now because you monkey-brains are slow learners, listen up.
One. Public art doesn't stop men pissing in public. Or make a freeway
    disappear.
Two. Public art that tries to avoid graffiti by pretend-copying graffiti
    doesn't fool anyone.
Three. If you must have figurative art, have dinosaurs. Not horses or
    humans.
Four. Unless you *are* Diego Rivera, avoid murals.
Five. Leave patriotism to the memorials.
And six. People generally prefer haphazard, complicated ruins—old
    dockyards and collapsed factories—over shiny plops of steel and
    sanitised plazas.

Impressed with my knowledge?
Well, could I tell you a bucketful—
if you stopped putting stupid tracking rings around my legs,
if you stopped pigeonholing me as sinister or malevolent.

I mean, stone me, how dare *Homo sapiens* criticise another species on
    moral grounds?
If I wanted to I could tell you
about the African moths living it up by the back door
about the missing girl's lake-coloured eyes...

A place with no name

I'm scratchland
I'm soured ditches and mangroves
I'm sapling and shrub
I'm a clockwork of deadwood
I'm the shadow under the bridge.

Avril Vas gazes from posters
sticky-taped to poles and shopfronts
it's a professional job a headshot
not a family snap or Instagram
Say cheese, big smile for the camera.

She's wearing spaghetti straps.
She was engaged.
She went to Los Angeles.
She wanted kids and to settle down.
She wanted to be an actress.

     A body.
     Female—tick.
     White—tick.
     Young, slim, blonde—tick, tick, tick.

First cops then the scientifics.
Words weave through the grass
with postmortem precision.

Loose ends rattle.
Acreage where bets are hedged
and feral dogs scrummage.

The splotch of the present tense.
In the spotlight's full glare
whoever you've become is unearthed.

    The story.
    Missing girl.
    Desperate family.
    Dusky suspects.

She's wearing spaghetti straps.
She was on the brink of stardom.
She was working in Starbucks.
She decided to stick it out in LA.
She decided to come home.

    A body.
    Semi-naked.
    One red shoe.
    She's a doll.

Pick up the doll
whose joints don't quite interlock
because her last hour on the line
the exhausted Chinese woman making it
was worrying about her sick father.

I'm a fingerprint.
I'm carpet fibre and creeping thistle.
I'm fungi becoming part of the undercurrent.
I'm the boat rocking gently.
I'm things that weren't supposed to happen.

Possible crime, underlying bass clarinet & a lesson in entomology

Suggested soundtrack
Eric Dolphy's *God Bless the Child (recorded live 1963).*

Mortification 101. A dead body supports a fast-changing ecosystem that takes it from flesh to bones in a matter of weeks—or months, depending on local geography.

> Flies are busy in her wounds
> rib-ends already exposed
> white beneath the black
> of dried muscle.

Different stages of decomposition attract different insect species. The first to arrive are the pioneers: blowflies and houseflies. They usually get there within twenty-four hours, but if there's blood or other bodily fluids leaking out, they can arrive in minutes. The adults lay their eggs, the eggs hatch into larvae. That's what maggots are: fly larvae.

> A missing girl
> a man in the picture
> the question nags
> what does his wife or girlfriend know?

The second wave of colonisation involves the sarcophagids or flesh flies. And when the fat of the corpse turns rancid, there's a third wave.

She's improvising
throwing in accidentals.

The cosmopolitan *Piophila casei* or cheese skippers constitute a
fourth wave. They aren't interested in the corpse when it's fresh,
but are attracted to the odour of the body in its later stages of
decomposition, especially during what's called butyric fermentation.

She gives it some lip
changes her tune.

Insects tend to work in a specific sequence. They usually lay their
eggs first in the facial orifices—unless there are wounds, in which
case they'll go there first, and then proceed down the body.

The girl's mother is ready to spill
the beans to tabloid TV
for the producer
this is ratings gold.

Of course, some have an altogether different game plan. Beetles, for
example. They're drawn not by the cadaver itself, but come to feed on
the other insects at the scene.

Coda (ritardando)
The amino acids
lysine and ornithine break down
proteins decompose
death stinks.

Solo for a cockroach

I'm not a helpful creature
or a useful one
I don't measure decay
or produce honey.

I turn up in your toaster
under the sink
I weave my reality into yours
inside the TV.

           I live in dark corners—of your homes

              your wastelands, your minds

I'm not by nature a storyteller

           I live for sex—that's pretty much it

             reproduction the bottom line

We're older than dinosaurs—
saw pterodactyls come and go
the first cockroach twitched onto the scene
three hundred million years before
the first flick of human history
I'm so much more than a nasty little pest.

Survival machines on six legs—that's us

an evolutionary masterpiece

I'm a natural superstar

You say yuck—or fuck

I respond with Latin polysyllables

We're members of the order Blattodea—
four-thousand species and still counting
a United Nations of cockroachkind
shit, soap, Styrofoam, sausage rolls
you name it I'll eat it
Let's say it again: I'm much more than a nasty little pest.

You'll find me in horror
in kiddie lit. and libraries
in entomology textbooks
sold secondhand for charity.

I inhabit an underworld
of traps and mop buckets
streams of Raid and services
bent on extermination.

I'm a defiant bastard, my alarm system fine-tuned—
antennae on my head
and
similar sensors at my arse-end
and
fact is most of us keep to ourselves
only a few species plague your kitchens
and
set up camp in cupboards
and
skitter through the maze of your life.

I take pride in my appearance—
thorax like lacquered mahogany
and
I keep myself clean
and
it may surprise you to know
I consider *H. sapiens* the hygiene problem—yes really.

back to sex—why not?

our sessions are marathons

lasting hours and even longer

Should I be reincarnated
I'd like to return as a writer
The Dreamlife of a Cockroach
my metamorphic riposte.

I'm the underdog—of the insect world

a bug in the system

but when humanity finally bites the dust

cockroaches will be there—to feast

on the remains

I really am so much more than a nasty little pest.

Mangroves & a shadowy past

I was Y
that was then
that was there
this is now
now I'm Jay.

My life stopped
I disappeared
like dial-up internet
now you see me
now I'm gone.

     Mangroves live life on the edge
     one foot on land one in the water.

First I made
the paperwork
story and then
I made myself
fit that story.

     Mangroves survive choking mud
     and salt levels that would kill most plants.

Once your origin
story is yanked out
by the roots
you've pressed the reset
button on yourself.

Mangroves are brilliant adapters
they shelter wildlife and buffer storms.

The surrounding murk sprouts aerial roots
as if someone's sown a crop of pencils.

Among the water-shadows and electronic yack
a sentence as long as a long haul flight.

Am I still the same
person inside?
what if you could
go all the way
and get a new inner life?

50-something woman

Occasions I'm given real-life flowers I put them in water with a
    half-teaspoon of bleach, then boil separate water for tea.
I toast two pieces of bread at the same time. It's less complicated than
    a single.
Life is complicated.
One slice reduced-fat cheese. Twenty grams no-sugar blackberry jam.
Make tea. Drink tea. Eat toast. Look at flowers.
Fight urge to check inbox or take long walk downhill
watch the flowers turn brown and putrefy
bite the head off a piece of broccoli.

Once upon a time in Walmart a security guard was trampled to
    death.
Two-thousand shoppers who'd queued overnight on the promise of a
    big deal sale smashed in the doors. Staff clambered onto vending
    machines to escape the stampede.
A security guard didn't make it.
When police arrived and declared the store a crime scene
shoppers were furious, they'd been waiting in the cold
over twenty-four hours to buy cheap stuff, and now
they're expected to go home
empty-handed!

Yvonne, 58, had a career. Now she's anonymous.
Ditto Ingrid, 55.
What are they supposed to do all day? Rearrange the furniture and
    binge on Scandi noir—angst and murder with added ice.
Watch cooking shows?
Rescue cats?

Volunteer for something?
Is this how ghosts feel?

It doesn't need a name. It's every fingernail you chew, every guideline
    that rules you out, every trip to the bathroom.
Frances, 50-something, goes to school. Parks hatchback. Enters staff
    room. Checks pigeonhole—full of the usual marketing brochures:
Shakespeare Made Easy.
Spelling Made Easy.
History Made Easy.
If it's all so easy, why is it so bloody hard?

I'm a 50-something woman who's been arrested—more than once.
Drink tea. Look at flowers.
To be, to be, a single me—that is the question.
Should I find someone online because it's easier to live in a twosome?
'He's a teacher too so you'll have a lot in common.'
Sit in the hairdresser's with foil on your head planning the next
    chapter:
Frances McRae, 50-something.
There is nothing more invisible than a middle-aged woman
nothing more discounted, more overlooked.

Once you're not young anymore and it's a battle
with extra kilos and crow's feet
and no one is going to give you flowers again, if they ever did to begin
    with...
You're in the queue—invisible.
You wait for the waiter—invisible.

You're ready to buy a new computer—invisible. The sales assistants
    are all tied up with blokes making important purchases
of twenty-dollar leads.

No wonder so many of us take up shoplifting—
it's the only way to get attention.
What's the most shoplifted item globally?
It's cheese.
Small, easy to slip into a bag or pocket.
Supermarket cheese isn't generally locked up or protected with
    security tags.
And it's a fair bet the CCTV cameras are trained on more valuable
    goods.
Drink tea. East toast. Look at flowers.

Did go on one date. Sat there stupid in candlelight
while he ran a monologue about cycling.
When were suburban roads emptied of playing children? You see a
    kid on a bike now and they're padded up and kitted out as if for
    combat.
I want to be told that I'm worth more than dog-walking and *Dr Phil*
and wasting time in that stupid charity shop
that I might be quite interesting if anyone could be bothered to find
    out
and that someone somewhere might actually want to fuck me.

Fight urge to check inbox or take long walk downhill.
Drink tea. Watch the flowers turn.
Decide life will not piss on my sparklers.

Drive to a rough-edge of town and—
Wow! Someone's cleared the litter
and carved out a garden
grevillea and herbs, a passionfruit vine, even water lilies.
Isn't that fantastic. Like Monet. What a gift!

Back to crow (& the storage clerk)

From the darksome night I come
I pilfer, I thieve, I risk the farmer's shotgun
to peck for leather-jackets and wireworms

From the darksome night I come
I ponder, I ask, I grapple with
questions earthy and philosophical

Are holes defined by what's around them?
Or is the thing that surrounds them defined by the hole?
Take a ring—I did. I hid that girl's ring
by a paperbark near the homeless camp
that was broken up after a murder back in the 1970s
(I'm sure you know the place I mean).

The metal in that band was made to fit
a woman with fingers of small circumference
almost child-sized—yes
it might be an engagement ring but
when I look at it I see two things: the gold band
and the emptiness inside.

When Caleb escapes
from schedules and realistics
he watches a YouTube bloke
measure radioactivity
in the ruins of Chernobyl
fish balloon in cooling ponds

corvids perch on silos
wolves den in unpeopled houses
moss shrouds everything.

From the darksome night I come
to show you the see-saw history
of this place (you know where I mean)
impromptu car park dash of cycle-path
the striking coal miners who hunted
rabbits for the pot in the winter of '49.

From the darksome night I come
I outwit, I tease, I play havoc
with your neoliberal logic.

Gone girls & thin lines

Down where the dirt road terminates
in lank weeds and stormwater grates

flash-flash-flash in the dying light
Joe Publics with iPhones drink up the sight.

Down where the dirt road terminates
blondes and redheads shine on upturned crates

reporters jostle to grab the best views
another gone girl hits the national news.

Down where the dirt road terminates
bloke with crunchy backstory awaits

is it some writer's dramatic nightmare
or true crime TV streaming live to air?

Storage clerk

Sandwich, side of chips, change of scene
getaway from Darren and his yarking.

Listen to this Caleb, did I tell you Caleb
wanna go down the Red Lion this weekend Caleb?

Lunch, look at nettles, stink bugs, moth vine
nothing to excite David Attenborough.

If you see these scratchlands on TV it's where
the deal goes bust or the cop goes over the edge.

This morning I was dealing with randoms—
That's correct, Sir. Storage unit rent is paid monthly in advance.
Yes, Madam, we have 24-7 security, yes that includes round-the-clock.
When the world ceases and heaven blows to the other side
of nowhere we'll always have storage.
Then up pops Darren with his social basketball and questions.
You still going out with what's-her-name, Caleb?

Her name's—never mind—and she's a shopaholic.
When we first got together she was fun.
Then she got a new job and had to upgrade her wardrobe.
And as she was promoted she upgraded again
and again, clothes, car, tea and coffee. Tea had to be green
and cappuccinos were a no-no. Strictly short black or macchiato.
Like she'd taken against milk.

What is it they're all so busy writing on those laptops?
People in cafés.
You can't get a seat because they're just sitting there
hours on end tapping away
writing novels or screenplays—or wanting everyone to think they are.
I mean, fuck, if they can afford four, five bucks a latte
you'd think they could afford wi-fi at home.

The upgrades continued until the only thing
she hadn't upgraded was me.
But I don't tell Darren any of that
I don't tell him how it all went pear-shaped
don't tell him I'd bought a ring
made a list of names for future kids
I just tell him: No.

She sustained minor bruising during an altercation
that word—altercation—who uses it except cops?
Hazmat, yellow tape, razor wire—they're the obvious
but there are more subtle ways. Anger keeps people away.

If you don't believe me have a meltdown. Try shouting
your head off somewhere public and watch people scatter.

I was so mad at her, for that day
for everything lately, for everything maybe ever.

Feral logistics

Muddles of seedheads and bunched ferns. We lock together and
become gully and common. We flow, a creek full of vomit water,
past the school with its demountables and off-key hymns. We're
plant successions, pollen and spore, entrails of earth, black-eyes
and berries so sour they kick the breath from your throat. We're the
clicking insects, scrubby concrete, a knotted stem in a shared root,
a harvest of black ink and block capitals. Keep Out, Trespassers Will
Be, Guard Dogs, etc.

Dumped computers reveal their trademark apples. We sink into
the fibre-optic mire, bashy rabbits, snakey cables, micro waves of
promises, most of them broken. We're the coding, the chemical
reaction, reality magnified, the light burning late in the lab. We're the
search going in circles, doubts seeping in, the fear that we may not
solve this one.

Let's go back to the plot with the laughter still inside the girl, the blow
still unstruck.

A translated life

I understood about fifty percent.
Conversations were out of focus.
Instead of hearing what people said
I watched their mouths
choreographies of hands and eyebrows.
Couldn't grasp the words but I heard voices
like musical instruments.
In seminars I imagined
I was part of a ramshackle orchestra
playing in and out of tune
that picked up a rhythm for a few bars

before losing it.

I went back last year for a visit.
Took me such a long time
to save for the aeroplane.
In Ouagadougou I visited relatives
bought *café au lait* from a wooden kiosk.
Watched a shoemaker fashion sandals
from old car tyres and went to the cinema.
The film was local with French subtitles
and although I understood the dialogue
it wasn't my language
the way it used to be

but the rhythm is still there.

Not so imaginary wolf

That's not the half of it, imagine
you're a canine, would you choose to live
wild and free as a wolf, or have a job with benefits,
like a sheep dog or police dog? Do as you're told,
put up with worming tablets and visits
to the vet sticking things up your whatsit.

Hotchpotch hybrids mishmash mongrels—
wolves and dogs, dogs and dingoes can interbreed, do it
all the time, but not with members of the extended family.
Our genetic make-ups are too different. Dingo and fox
would be like a human mating with
a chimpanzee. Not gonna work.

Might appear hairy but we're harmless wouldn't squash
a flea. Our histories—detailed and dramatic as Nordic sagas—
have taken a tragic turn. Oops! She fell, fingers and thumbs,
banged her head. Blood. Engagement ring. Smile!
Somewhere close by, a twig snaps. Don't turn
your back on me, love.

Fucking Hansel. Fucking Gretel. Sweet-tooth kids—No,
let's go with the trees, where bush joins town
like a shadow attaches to a heel. Way more
interesting than those whiny little bastards.
Somewhere close by, a twig snaps. Don't turn
your back on me, love.

I spy with my wolf-eye something beginning
with a gingerbread house, the silence
of an empty foodbowl, a shooting script. Teddy stabbed
with kitchen scissors, words pulled
from mouths like hair from the drain. Don't turn
your back on me, love.

NB
We're not an individualistic species. But the pack-memory of *Canis
lupus* is profound.

Crossed wires & mixed messages

It's me again.

After the fire
there's only wire.
Bed springs, fly screens
filaments, coils, bits of machines.
That's all we've got left
fucking useless bloody wire.

Hey Caleb, it's Darren just wondering.

I'm calling from Save the World's Children.

Me again.

Take me through the moment.

You can't trust pixels.
I'm a ghost from an earlier filming.
I was in the last shot
and when it was recorded over
it didn't completely erase me.
You get that in CCTV.
That's why I'm in the picture, OK?

I'll try you later.

Would you mind answering a few questions?

What is hummus Mister? she asked.
So I told her
nothing unnatural.
There were blisters on her arms
the circumference of cigarette ends.
Mosquito bites she said
and scratched them until they bled.
She said they ate legs from KFC
Mum and Bob's-her-uncle in front of the TV.
So I told her
at the spice bazaar in Eminönü
vendors slice up fifty kinds of cheese.
I told her
about the Bosphorus where the blue is supple
the day ends with a comma
and all that is solid melts into money.

It just happened.

Hi, this is Frances, I can be reached.

Sometimes we do things and feel things we shouldn't. Sorry.

I'm following up to see if you're still in the market.

Hello sweetheart.
We haven't heard from you in a while
and with Gareth's twenty-first coming up,
well, we thought, your dad and me—

if you need help with the fare give me a call.
Give us a call anyway Avril.
Your dad worries about you
we both do.
Give us a call when you get this...

The fact of an event
leads us backwards.
We struggle
to find cause
when perhaps there isn't one.
That desire to couple effect and cause
takes us down well-trodden paths
and we lose sight of the myriad other paths
that might have brought us to this point.

Mongrel

At first Jay was uninterested
to the point of repulsion—or close.
X was everything
he'd come to despise.
Jay thought of himself
as suave, discreet.
X was common
body-type that would run to fat—in time.
There was nothing discreet about X
but neither was there anything mean
and over time Jay grew to appreciate
the beauty of a big heart
and he fell in love with X
deeply, totally, indiscreetly in love.

Some of my best friends are dogs.

Scenario for a busted piano & various wrongdoings

Car drives into a rough patch.
Something is thrown out
car speeds off.
Dog barks.

Starts to rain.
Drops land on exposed strings
of a broken piano.
Eerie percussion.

Fox scat, fish scales
bike frames, hufflepuff
pin drops.
A heart stops.

In her story there's a forest
and in the clearing
creatures with heavy paws.
Someone's crying.

> Typical kids, bilingual, sometimes stoned,
> sometimes athletic, first-generation
> kids whose parents are still enflamed
> by the past that drove them here.

> Now a darling, now a druggie,
> a zombie, a sweetie.
> Inconsolable, crying for days—
> What happened was awful.

Soon this plot will disappear.

Bulldozers move in.

Only the stories remain

and after a while

they too disappear.

Soundtrack for Scratchland

Key instruments:
Bass clarinet, clarinet, toy piano.

The Beatles: 'When I'm Sixty-four' (*Sgt. Pepper's Lonely Hearts Club Band*)

Anouar Brahem Trio: 'Aube rouge à Grozny' (*Astrakan café*)

Don Byron: 'I Want to be Happy' (*Ivey-Divey*)

Don Byron: 'Lefty Teachers at Home' (*Ivey-Divey*)

Eric Dolphy Quintet: 'Green Dolphin Street' (*Eric Dolphy Quintet*)

Eric Dolphy: 'God Bless the Child' (*The Illinois Concert*)

Eric Dolphy: 'Something Sweet, Something Tender' (*Out to Lunch*)

Barabos Erköse: 'Hüzzam Keman Taksimi' (*Aşkın Yolu*)

Margaret Leng Tan: 'Modern Love Waltz' (*The Art of the Toy Piano*)

Margaret Leng Tan: 'Dream, For Piano' (*She Herself Alone: The Art of the Toy Piano 2*)

Sqwonk: 'KlezDuo (*Sqwonk*)

Jason Stein's Locksmith Isidore: 'As Many Chances as You Need' (*After Caroline*)

Jason Stein Quartet: 'Work' (*The Story This Time*)

Tiago Videira: 'Bean Soup' (*Toy Portugal*)

Edmund Welles: 'When I Woke Up, Everyone Was Gone' (*Imagination Lost*)

True crimers

I

I confess: guilty as charged. I'm an addict. Started small time with regular programs. A procession of moody, idiosyncratic, music-loving British detectives. Until fictional murders in chocolate-box villages or on windswept moors weren't doing it for me, giving me the rush I needed. I wanted tougher shit. Mug shots, contusions, clinical descriptions. I wanted real-life suspects. I wanted blame. I wanted true crime exposés. And before you know it, I'm hooked on this stuff. Night after night sitting on the couch gorging on the misfortune of strangers. The fuck-ups of the justice system. Yes, it's an unhealthy diet, yes, I know it's bad for me. (BTW I have tried to kick the habit. Gone cold turkey, once lasted almost three weeks.) Truth is though, it helps me escape from the general crappiness of the world even as it's showing me that crappiness in all its brutal, brain-bashed, haphazard detail. What can I say? OMG lead me not into TV.

II

It happens in somebody else's house. It happens in an American nowhere where nothing changes, but when it does, it's for the worse. It happens across town. It's not my window lifted, it's not my loser, crackhead ex-boyfriend creeping in while I'm asleep. It's not me delivered into a machete with great force. It's not my body broken into pieces like a pomegranate. It's someone else's horror. In my house they're just images on television.

Winter acquires an extra cold shiver when blonde, blue-eyed Carson Howe is found hacked to death in her home. With no sign of forced entry, police believe that Carson knew her attacker—until a witness comes forward with a clue that leads to an angry, revenge-hungry killer.

It's them, Carson Howe's family, not mine counting down the first 48 hours...

III

Sawn-off small talk, roughcast charm, routine is fine, pays on time,
keeps a tidy house. Bit of peacocking, but what bloke doesn't? Let's
face it, sex and romance are the only sources of adventure open to
most of us. And at the bottom of that pit are the terrors of being
beige, being someone nothing ever happens to. Run-of-the-mill
job, boring mortgage, kids, you live your life on the safe side and
look where it gets you. Mind you...He's a good talker—did I already
say that?

IV

I don't understand that blind loyalty to a man. If things were the
other way around he'd throw you to the wolves. Slap, slap, slap,
waves hit the jetty. This one's not a short-fuse merchant, or a singlet-
wearing stereotype. He's an everybloke with a boat. The kind of man
we trust.

A coastal town was shocked when reports came in that real estate
agent Alex McKendrick had fallen overboard into the deep dark
of the ocean. Months passed, details evaporated...the mystery
remained. Will new DNA technology finally reveal what happened on
that yacht?

They may be a complete waste of space with a history of violence
long as your arm, but from the mouths of their mates and relatives
come the inexorable platitudes. Salt of the earth, generous to a fault,
wouldn't harm a fly. So I killed him. I killed the controlling bastard.

V

I absolutely don't see it as murder porn. I'm first and foremost a storyteller. I do cop a lot of flack though. I get accused of exploitation, fear-mongering, of exposing society's ratty underwear. To which I reply: No, No and Someone's got to. Look, I get it: my protagonists are ethically challenged, they're not nice people, but there are bugs in the legal machinery. If I think it's a wrongful conviction or the case rests on dodgy evidence, yes, I do go in with a certain slant. I'm a journalist and my job is to hold the system accountable.

Push comes to shove I'm making programs for a wide audience which means you dramatise aspects to help viewers understand them. The sweet girl with big dreams, the perfect wife, the divorcee looking for a second act. Human brittleness laid bare. I think of true crime as the adult equivalent of fairy tales for kids. There's menace but you experience it from the safety of the sofa. Sure I shape the narrative, but I'm not a character in it, I'm a conduit.

VI

Ladies, Girls, here's the shit. Your skirt's so short, your heels so high. You totter to the bar for another rum and Coke, clickety-clack like a ticking clock. You and your girl-mates are on the scout. Yeah, hope's a bitch. It nags at you, bumps up your drinking, and now the night is black as weeds and there's a ute turning onto a dirt road...But all that's to come. For now I'm your Romeo, your Casanova, your man of the moment. Ladies tonight is your lucky night! Tick-tock. Everybody has a future but some have more than others.

VII

I'm up late with a cold case. In the kitchen last week's milk is quietly
expiring. I need something sweet while bodies are exhumed. A hit of
caffeine to keep me awake. I can't be stuffed to go the extra half-mile
so it's the all-nighter on the corner. Chocolate, pet food, sticky tape
six-bucks a roll—and serendipity. The episode I'm watching kicks
off with a killing in a 7-Eleven. Cut to vox pop from shocked locals
insisting it isn't a bad neighbourhood, but it has elements. That's how
they phrase it. Elements.

They're unfriendly places convenience stores. Overseas students
glued to their iPhones. Over-priced snacks and over-the-top security.
Go in grab a litre and a Kit Kat sharepack then back home to the
violent small hours. Eyeballs like lychees. Multiple fractures. A few
bars of suitably sombre music then back to the chorus of residents.
We all muddle along. Relative harmony, blah, blah, blah. Community
can be such a mush.

VIII

I know what it's like to grow up an orchid-house only child. Three in the family makes a triangle—sharp angles, pointy corners. I longed for siblings to soften the geometry.

Our team leader's jokes overshoot their punchlines. His voice coarse and patchy like a clarinet with a bung reed. I zone out. The meeting rattles on. I start drawing a circle on my agenda. Circles are neutral. Beginnings and endings all rolled into one, never stopping, never starting. Going down then coming back up again. My pen keeps moving, round and round, consolidating the circumference. Then spins off to make new circles. Perfect circles lucid as engagement rings.

That's when it comes to me. How I might acquire the sisters and brothers my parents denied me. How I might put some storm in my hitherto three-sided life.

IX

What's on the surface may not be as superficial as it seems. That's security thinking. Once upon a time I was a detective sergeant, now I consult.

The ex had her under surveillance. She didn't have an inkling of course. If she'd been firing on all cylinders she'd have asked herself how come Christina always knew where she was, who she'd spoken with at the gym, who she'd texted. But she was stressed out. Custody dispute, impending court case, etc.

How can you tell if you're being monitored?

Step one. Listen. Sometimes you can hear the tiny, clicking sound cameras make when they're activated. Turn off electrical appliances, get the place as silent as you can. See if you pick up anything.

Step two. Overnight. When the room is submerged in full darkness shine a torch around the space. Pay attention to corners, architraves, smoke alarms. Watch for reflections or glints where there shouldn't be any.

X

They filmed me in the staff room. Tidied up the notices about subcommittees and cake mornings. Tempted me with prosecco and a cheese plate. Blue vein, Swiss, something artisan and runny. You taught him history, Frances—can I call you Frances? What was he like? I'd already told her in our pre-interview chat that I barely remembered him. *A skinny lad with hair the colour of a polished two-dollar coin.* Her TV smile went down a few watts. I'm more interested, Frances, in what he was like mentally. Were there early signs of the violence to come? I tried to hit the right note. *On the other side of the school fence, you might hear differently, but in the classroom he kept his head down. I don't recall any trouble.* Then it stands to reason, she said, that something happened to make him lose it. I don't say this to camera, but I know that isn't always so. Some kids get lost all by themselves with no apparent trigger. An assistant thanked me for my participation with a gift-pack of scented candles. Bloody scented candles! Just one last question, Frances, if that's OK. Did you ever hear from him after he'd left school? *No. But I saw him once. He was buying a tin of baked beans.* We were in one of those over-bright convenience stores. He seemed lethargic, out of it. There were no beans in him.

It all went wrong. It wasn't his fault. In his heart he was a gentle soul, not a killer. She pushed him into it. Good as. Unable to manage her disappointment she grew spiteful. Bills were piling up, she threw them in his face. He felt humiliated. Yes, he had a gambling problem—who doesn't? In any case at about 5:00 am in that purplish light that flares before dawn Fenton Xavier held up a convenience store. Killing the sales guy was never part of his plan. It just happened.

At this point my sympathy lies with Fenton.

Henpecked, hounded Fenton. Full of poor white blood cells. And now scared that his wife, Dee, would inform. He had to eliminate that possibility. Permanently. No choice. On the 17 April Fenton bludgeoned Dee to death with a claw hammer. She was seven months pregnant.

A few words about lives upended by poverty and debt, and now the program presenter is interviewing Fenton's sister and brother-in-law. He's not a monster. They don't wish to speak ill of the dead but Dee was a narcissistic sociopath. Everyone adds their two cents' worth of junk psychology.

By now I've lost any lingering sympathy—or should that be empathy?—I had for Fenton.

Empathy is a recent addition to the English lexicon. It goes beyond sympathy which has been around a few centuries longer. Empathy is more first person. It's someone else's shoes. We use the two words synonymously but I've noticed that these days empathy is heaps more popular than sympathy.

Found God when I was inside, didn't I? Reformed character. Up before the parole board: Please sir, I'm very sorry. I've let Jesus into my life and he's taught me to be a good boy.

What separates law-abiders from crims? To the choir of the self-righteous I say it's a narrow margin. Anyone who's ever smoked a joint or snorted a line is in the grey zone.

Mum was a basket case. Me and my sister ended up in foster care. When I was fourteen I crashed a car we'd nicked. Came out of the accident with occipital neuralgia. That's what the medics call it. I call it fucking unfair.

Gives me terrible, electrical headaches. Legit pills eased the pain a bit but not enough, specially on black hole days when I just want to lie down and die. I needed booze and outside drugs as well. But when I cocktailed all that stuff some inner demon escaped. I've always had a crust on me and that day I was blinking and blinking like a mental job but everything stayed out of focus.

The presenter's face seems vaguely familiar. Blonde hair, shiny teeth, red top, tits straining at the fabric. Makes me furious. I hurl the remote at the television. It hits the screen with a thud. The TV flashes, spreading light over the walls and the hundreds of photos covering them.

God help you.

True crime is hot. True. A recent development. Not true. Go back to the Victorian era and people were just as hungry for it. Sensational reports in daily newspapers, the serial fiction-inspired-by-fact of Charles Dickens or Wilkie Collins.

Now we hoard the gory details in podcasts and docos.

I'm Florence Ishikawa. I lecture in media and cultural studies. My PhD addressed true crime as a pop culture phenomenon. Sharp-force injuries, toxicology reports, the horror next door but one. Who watches true crime TV? A furtive audience of lurkers and pasty-face blokes in basements. Not true again. Research indicates the fanbase is predominantly female.

Is it all vicarious buzz or does re-enacting the event and its aftermath contribute to our understanding of crime and punishment? In court the accused has an opportunity to contest the charges. In these programs—not so much. Critics of the genre argue that it asks the wrong questions. Focuses on individual stories instead of systemic problems like inequality, corruption, climate change, human rights. True. And not true. These are large-scale issues, social crimes if you like, that we seem unable or unwilling to resolve. Drilling down on one case and following it through to some kind of conclusion helps us feel we have agency in our own lives.

I often get asked if I like true crime TV. I do. But I also enjoy untrue crime. Miss Marple. I love her curiosity and how she's always knitting. I love that every time she goes anywhere, whether it's the Caribbean or central London, a person must die. I love the meandering revelations of the mystery, as a woman easily dismissed as a dotty old bat, reveals whodunnit.

What's your favourite amino acid? Mine's valine. Body-builders like it because it promotes muscle growth, but I like its origin story. It was identified in 1901 by a German chemist who had a stellar career but a heartbreaking personal life. Alanine, arginine, asparagine—only four years since uni, but it feels a lifetime. The counsellor came up with the idea. Lists to keep a lid on my anxiety. Amino acids, fruit and vegetables A to Z, silences. The silence that follows a car crash. The silence that greets unwelcome news. The silence of an unplayed piano. The silence of the house at night. Ear-shattering silence. The silence of unanswered questions. The silence that makes mysteries of the stars.

Butterfly: Hi there Loverhead.
Loverhead: Hey Butterfly! You made it.
Butterfly: I managed to wrangle an early break. Hope I'm not missed back at the office.
Loverhead: What do you do?
I'd anticipated this question.
Butterfly: Admin for a small business.
Keep it vague. I don't want him to track me down. I'm not even sure how far I want the relationship to go. I'm just happy to have an online connection with a cool guy. Someone who won't see thunder thighs Siobhan Connor-Harding, thirteen years old, hopeless at sport and not very good at academic subjects either.
Loverhead: I guess you spend hours in front of a computer.
Butterfly: It's OK. I get to go overseas. I fly a lot. I went to a trade fair in Singapore last December and got upgraded.
Better tone it down. Don't want to sound like I'm boasting.
But most of the time, I'm stuck in the office.
Loverhead: No such fun for me. I'm in computers. Sounds way more impressive than it is in reality. Fancy chatting again?

Mum has no idea. She came into my bedroom when I was watching *Love Island* glanced at it for thirty seconds and passed judgement. Said it was all manufactured by the program producers. I ignored her. The people on the show aren't actors, they're real! My favourites are the romantic ones like *First Dates* and *The Bachelorette*.

Loverhead: How's it going?
Butterfly: Feeling a bit low. Some girls are being really mean.
Loverhead: Lucky you've got me then. I love talking to you. You're the cutest, nicest person I've met on this site. Would you like to meet IRL?
With a ton of make up and skyscraper stilettos I reckon I can pass for eighteen.
Butterfly: I could meet you outside the park main gate, about five thirty.
Smiling emoji.
Loverhead: I'll be waiting.

XVI

Air scratchy as fibreglass, an ooze of dead leaves, the scuffing of a helicopter. Leftover spaces, sour places, life in the outtakes. Now a suburban street. Now a dark alley and the young woman is walking down it towards a thoroughfare vivid with lights and roofed with stars. 'Reconstruction' pops up in the top right corner of the screen.

Most of my favourite stuff is American: cheeseburgers, iPads, the Investigation Discovery network. College student and aspiring actress Nicola McCabe goes missing after her car swerves off a lonely road on the outskirts. As months pass her family and friends refuse to give up their quest to find out what happened that fateful midsummer night.

Stray hairs, loose threads, the nitty gritty of forensics. Talking heads in dimly lit kitchens. Bombshells, skin cells, gut feelings. Now a journalist. Now a psychologist telling the same old story of boundless rage against the female sex. Satellite connections transmit dramas of death and disappearance into unsuspecting skies.

XVII

My name is Sara Basic—that's Baz-itch not fundamental. Somewhere in the journey from Croatia to here it dropped its diacritics. I'm a recently divorced casual teacher. ESL—English as a second language. Helping recent immigrants imagine a better life for themselves while they slog it out in the gig economy. Unfortunately teaching work has dried up which means right now I'm a live-in dog-sitter. That's kind of embarrassing so I tell people I'm researching a novel. And I am, I'm watching a lot of crime, mostly of the 'true' variety but when I need closure I switch over to fiction.

The men in my life, yes, come and go. The SIO (Senior Investigating Officer) arrives, flashes his ID and ducks under the police tape. The FME (Forensic Medical Examiner) gets out of his BMW. A stutter of blue and red lights punctuates the dark and attracts nearby residents in PJs and dressing gowns. Dialogue is brief and to the point. TOD (Time of Death)? Probable cause? Best guess: blunt force trauma. He'll know more after the PM (Post Mortem). By the end of the program, and not without several close shaves, the lead detective will have arrested the perp.

XVIII

Seven, eight, late as ten or eleven o'clock sometimes. He's at work all
hours. Last-minute meetings. Mind you, lots of families are like that
nowadays, aren't they? I'm not saying there's any funny business.
He needs some room in his life that's just his. Does that make sense?
I straighten the cushions. Dust crystalware and china women who
stare into space. In the garden ivy pushes its holdfasts into rifts and
crevices. Insidious at first, then impossible to ignore. And here's the
thing—if I rip it out it'll leave cracks in the masonry that will never
close. Not completely.

XIX

Trust me, the urgings of the heart can be fucking cruel. Look in the mirror. I see two eyes shiny as glass, I see an animal stalking its prey. I see blackthorn and suckers.

Had to let me go, didn't they. Evidence was all circumstantial—meaning there's more than one explanation for its existence.

Way I understand it everybody's got their own head-tune. It plays on a loop in your brain and nothing, no meds, no psychs, no do-gooders with their quinoa salads and yoga, nothing can erase that tune. Ninety-nine percent of people's head-tunes are mellow, but mine, mine is discordant. It drives me nuts. The only thing that gets rid of the fucking noise is—well, you know what it is.

XX

I thought he was too good to be true. And he was. We'd been together a few months and till then his whole persona had been carefully crafted. Always considerate, always respectful, bit of a coiled spring, bit brooding, but always quick to compose himself and apologise.

I'm a huge *Jane Eyre* fan—love the old 1943 film with Orson Welles. I cast him as a twenty-first century Mr Rochester.

And then one day without warning he went incandescent—

He completely lost it when he opened his lunch box and discovered a fruit slice with seeds in it. If you fucking feed me any more fucking seeds— You'll what, I laughed, desperate to defuse the situation, start chirping?

Scenario 1. Words spew in bubbles of blood. There's a boot on my neck and I'm being forced down. My face smacks against the tiles. Air is forced from my lungs, bile fills my mouth...'*I desired liberty; for liberty I gasped; for liberty I uttered a prayer.*'

Scenario 2. Reader, I left him.

XXI

The stories are icky. But thrilling. You roller-coast between guilt and reasonable doubt. The more you watch the more you notice things that don't add up. Cover-ups. Watchdogs, underdogs. You get to know the cast. Retired cops, reporters, the broken-hearts, the psychologicals and the science-y types who collect butts, condoms and other yuck. Those will be checked for prints and other identifiers. And sometimes you've got to laugh. One geeky-looking expert drones on and on about blowflies like he's in love with them or something.

Specialists join the spatter of blood dots.

I think about all the ways we can be wrong.

In front of the camera, confusion and damage gel into a story that begins with a teenage mother and petty theft. To be honest in a lot of true-crime shows the end is clear from the start. Is that what you call a classic?

I'm never going into an underground car park at night. I'm never going near that scrappy patch of trees and I'm definitely not going into the forest. I'm not going camping just me and him and nature. I'm not going to deliver a basket of food to an old woman. I'm never going to accept a lift from an online hook-up. I'm never going to let myself be tricked by some sly old wolf. Should I ever find myself 'helping the police with their inquiries' and they offer me coffee or a drink of water I certainly won't be stupid enough to accept. How many times have we seen that a glass is a transparent attempt to get DNA from saliva? No way. Not going to happen.

I'm a results woman. My name is Wendy Furtado, I'm six months shy of fifty, a few pounds overweight, and I'm a pathologist. A plant pathologist. I study the organisms and environmental conditions that cause disease in plants. I generally work with government bodies on matters of agriculture or biosecurity, but occasionally I get called in to help with a homicide. My role there is to make connections between botanical evidence and the crime. Put the clues of the natural world under the microscope. A fungal or bacterial disease can tie an individual or object to a specific location.

The child went missing at the beginning of winter. When they found his body, his clothing yielded traces of vegetal material. Leaf scraps showed signs of myrtle rust, a disease not present in the area where the boy was buried. I was able to demonstrate that the pathogen strain obtained from this sample collected at the crime scene was a taxonomic match to that found hundreds of kilometres distant at a suspect's property.

Cucumber Green Mottle Mosaic Virus has a poetic ring but it's a nasty disease that affects the cucurbit family—pumpkin, zucchini, watermelon, et al. That's my current research. What else can I tell you? There's been talk of a TV program inspired by my work. My Head of Department is impressed by that. I'm not. And it's a job where striking the right balance between being a pushover and a push-aside is tough. Especially for women.

XXIV

I wanted to be a celebrity so badly that I could taste it. And it tasted like blood. It was a painful, all-consuming desire and the fact that I wasn't famous hurt more, not less, because I so nearly was. YouTube, Instagram, scores of #hashtags. What I craved wasn't so much money as consequence. I wanted to be undeletable.

The show opens with a close-up. A selfie of an attractive brunette. Then another photo of the same young woman, this time in a bikini, this time tongue out, licking an ice cream. Next true-crime author Dylan Anders appears, bookcase out of focus in the background, and explains how he became obsessed with this murder. (It's something to do with the combination of the girl's beauty and the horrific reality of her death.)

XXV

Start at the start. Debit Mastercard declined. Facts helpful, emotions less so. Joint account balance $7. I wondered if he'd got into online gambling, so I searched his computer. Accessing his email account proved simpler than anticipated. I considered what was most important to him before typing in his mother's name (Patricia) and birthday. It's surprising how many people use that method to create a password. The tech guy at work told me that. He'd worked in cybersecurity and knew all about sequences and passwords. He cracked mine in a few minutes, guessing correctly that I'd used the dog's name (Growly) and my house number (141).

Credit cards maxed out. Our finances were in the toilet. He was sending money and designer gear to a girl he'd met on a business trip to the Philippines. Not to mention gooey messages of love and lust. I don't feel angry, I feel like—I feel like a cucumber. Made of water. I know that sounds ridiculous, but I do, I feel full of it.

Practicalities first. Bank. Assets. Change passwords. Deep breath. No more tears for what was or might have been.

Outside laburnum blossom hangs in yellow sheets, sweetly toxic.

Patricia indulged, flattered and protected her son until his opinion of his own importance lost all touch with reality.

People can be extremely good at keeping secrets when we need to.

I told Growly my plan.

'A' shot B in the head. 'A' was a misfit weirdo. B was beloved by all.
And so it goes. Twenty-eight year old Lulu Woźniak left a barbecue
party and fell out of the story. Police investigating a house fire make
a gruesome discovery. True Crime Trudi—that's me. Eat pizza,
drink New Zealand sav blanc, talk of karma and just desserts. But
don't assume my appetite for these programs means I swallow them
holus-bolus. I have insights. For example, have you noticed the role
locations play?

The slurp of a creek. The end of the road. The kind of place teenagers
go to drink and fuck. It's where cops found a bloodstained hoodie.
Also found, one gold ring. Girl-size.

If it's scenic, cue shock and horror. Leafy street, beautiful
beachside—how could such savagery happen here? If it's shabby or
rundown the implication swings the other way. What do you expect
in a shithole like this?

Pretty country town. Hymns leak from church halls. The kind
of place newlyweds go to start a family. It's where cops found a
bloodstained hoodie. Also found, one gold ring. Girl-size.

I ask the questions. Usually. Today though, I'm on the other side of the table giving answers for a true crime reality show. I'm treading cautiously, minding my p's and q's because these programs love to point the finger at our shortcomings. The interviewer, a trim-looking older bloke with gelled hair, asks me to introduce myself. *Ghassan Khoury, Detective Constable. Everyone calls me Ghaz.* Neroli Mason and her four-year-old son were executed inside their house. You were one of the first officers on the scene. What were your impressions? I remember a moth-eaten teddy bear, a bag of corn chips open on the settee, petechial haemorrhaging in dead eyes. But I keep those images to myself and state the obvious: *There was a strong smell of bleach. Thanks to TV every Tom, Dick and axe murderer knows bleach thwarts CSIs.* Someone off camera calls a five-minute break. Over coffee I wonder whether programs like this one encourage people to believe there are no shades of grey. Only varying depths of black. The interview resumes. I understand the husband gave the police a description? I don't intend to broadcast this, but Eddie Mason was a right dickhead biscuit. His so-called evidence led us down a series of blind alleys. *We needed to locate Mrs Mason's phone.* Had it been stolen? *No, it had slipped down the back of a cupboard. We had to coax it out with a length of wire.* That's what bedevils most investigations. Not the lies, not the straight-out fairy tales, but the inadvertent sloppiness of the day-to-day.

XXVIII

Fear of catfish. Fear of dating apps and dogs. Fear of looking. Fear of looking foolish. Fear of calories and country towns. Fear of breaking down. Fear of ivy and other creepers. Fear of black birds and bus depots, especially at night. Fear of soccer dads with irregular kids. Fear of unwanted photography. Fear of adjectives. Fear of fear, of fucking everything.

XXIX

A woman had been dismembered. Lori-ann suspected her fiancé was involved, although he emphatically denied it. Either way, it was her duty to provide him with an alibi.

On screen, I've been adapted. I'm slim and smart. Ambitious too, and of course young. I'm a hot-shot journalist who keeps super fit by jogging in the surrounding woods. A city girl, I rock up to this small town in my flash car and prod old wounds. The townsfolk regard me with suspicion. I ask for pinot noir in the local bar. Despite the fact that no one really wants to talk to me, I manage to learn more about the murder. A maverick cop shares details of the dismemberment and lets me see photos of the crime scene. What I don't realise is that I myself am in danger—the killer's got me in his sights. One evening the lock on my front door is forced and before I can scream for help, he's dragged me into his vehicle. In the adaptation, I kill my captor and escape. In reality the story returns to the past tense and becomes another cautionary tale.

XXX

If you were a medieval person chances are you'd have met a devil. Every hedge, hailstone, hotel and hamlet harboured some kind of threat.

He was such a happy kid, always laughing. He was our little angel.

Don't forget: Satan was an angel before he got expelled from heaven.

He had a larrikin streak and he could be a bit of a nuisance, but he was a good boy.

Demons opened trapdoors, hid in jugs of beer and imperilled mortal souls.

We reassure ourselves that we know our children, that they'll turn out maybe not model citizens, but basically OK.

You have to understand not only the nature of evil, but the extravagance of tricks by which evil masquerades as normal.

The more adult he grew, the less we knew about our son. Somewhere along the line he lost his balance and cruelty seeped into all the cracks of his being.

Dealing with human beings you never know everything, not even when you know everything there is to know.

Acknowledgements

This one has been a slow burn. 'Scenarios & solos from a mixed landscape', the first part of *Scratchland*, was researched and written to first draft as part of a Creative Fellowship from the University of Queensland. It was subsequently workshopped at Yale University as part of the Windham-Campbell Literary Festival.

Heartfelt thanks to Terri-ann White and the team at UWA Publishing for their commitment to new Australian writing, and whose fabulous work has made this book possible. To my 7-ON colleagues (Donna Abela, Vanessa Bates, Hilary Bell, Verity Laughton, Ned Manning and Catherine Zimdahl) for all things playwriting and way beyond. To directors Ian Lawson in Brisbane and Margot Bordelon in the USA. To agents Lisa Fagan and Anthony Blair at Cameron Creswell. To Professor Joanne Thompkins and Dr Stephen Carleton at the University of Queensland. And to my partner, writer and film-maker Kathryn Millard, for her creative insights, big-picture thinking and everything else. Endless gratitude all round.